HELP IS ON THE WAY

And Love Is Already Here

JONATHAN MARTIN

ZONDERVAN

Help Is on the Way
Copyright © 2016 by Jonathan Martin

Requests for information should be addressed to:
Zondervan, 3900 *Sparks Dr. SE, Grand Rapids, Michigan* 49546

ISBN 978-0-310-34658-6 (booklet)

ISBN 978-0-310-34664-7 (ebook)

Unless otherwise noted, Scripture quotations are taken from
the *New Revised Standard Version Bible*. Copyright © 1989
National Council of the Churches of Christ in the United States
of America. Used by permission. All rights reserved.

Scripture quotations marked NIV are from The Holy Bible, New
International Version®, NIV®. Copyright © 1973, 1978, 1984, 2011
by Biblica, Inc.® Used by permission of Zondervan. All rights
reserved worldwide. www.Zondervan.com. The "NIV" and "New
International Version" are trademarks registered in the United
States Patent and Trademark Office by Biblica, Inc.®

All of the text in this booklet is taken from *How to Survive a
Shipwreck*. Copyright © 2016 by Jonathan Martin.

All rights reserved. No part of this publication may be
reproduced, stored in a retrieval system, or transmitted in any
form or by any means—electronic, mechanical, photocopy,
recording, or any other—except for brief quotations in printed
reviews, without the prior permission of the publisher.

Published in association with the literary agency of D. C.
Jacobson and Associates LLC, an Author Management
Company. www.dcjacobson.com.

Cover design: Curt Diepenhorst
Cover photography: Shutterstock
Interior design: Kait Lamphere

First Printing April 2016 / Printed in the United States of America

Contents

Deep calls to deep at the roar of your
waterfalls;
    all your breakers and your waves
        have gone over me.

Psalm 42.7

the tempest
the darkness
the waves that you sent
just the saltwater taste
of these songs of descent

still sinking
still losing
the waves won't relent
I won't go down quiet
this is a song of dissent.

no flailing
no swimming
I'm not innocent
water fills my lungs
This is my song of descent.

Chapter One

Losing Your Ship without Losing Your Soul

Only those who are lost will find the promised land.

Rabbi Abraham Heschel

We are all in the same boat, in a stormy sea, and we owe each other a terrible loyalty.

G. K. Chesterton

The experience of drowning, through the lens of faith, is what Christians call "baptism." But no matter what you call it, the sensation of going under is entirely the same.

It was Easter Sunday at the church I founded in my hometown. I had preached on the first words of Jesus when he appeared to the disciples after his resurrection: "Do not be afraid."[1] I said

5

you could sum up the whole of God's message to humans throughout Scripture and throughout history in those four words—*Do not be afraid*. I told our people these are words that are spoken when it would seem to us we have every reason in the world to be afraid. That God speaks them when he is about to do something new. And in the midst of this sermon on death and resurrection, I announced I was leaving.

I felt like I was the pastor who stole Easter.

Of course, there was a part of me that felt ridiculous announcing my departure on the Sunday with the biggest attendance of the year, when everybody has dressed up and brought their friends. But I was not going to keep grabbing every rung of the ladder on the way down, trying to salvage the unsalvageable. I was not going to stay plugged into the ventilator. The only message I could preach was the only message my life could be at that point, and it was the message of death and resurrection.

Painful as it was, I knew this had to be my last sermon. I could not drag the ending out any further. I was over. I told my congregation I would be there the next Sunday for a transition service, but I would not preach again. The message of death and resurrection had finally grabbed hold of me, not in the way it grabs hold of a preacher but in the way it grabs hold of a man. I had no idea what I was walking into. I was stepping into a starless night. I only knew it was time to cash in all my chips on the hope that resurrection could be a better existence than the one I was sort of maintaining.

At the conclusion of both services, I baptized people for the last time at this church I had founded and given my life to. I felt the holiness of each of them as I gently lowered their bodies into the water, the tour guide for their own descent. I was almost done baptizing people when Heather came out of her pew with lips quivering, her face contorted in anguish. We had just buried her father, Herman, a few weeks before, and everything about his early departure was filled with ambiguity. It had been a torturous ride for her—the ordeal of her father's fall, the many hours in the hospital, the celebration that he was better and resuming normal life, the second tragic turn that led to serious decline, the weight of the decision to pull the plug.

Heather kicked off her flip-flops when she got down front and practically threw her cell phone onto the stage. As she took off her glasses and I helped her into the pool, it was not the cherubic look of a new convert on her face, excited about new faith in Jesus. It was a mix of resignation, heartbreak, an almost angry determination, and yet a kind of hope too that if she could jump into the river that carries us toward death, there could be new life for her too. Already, my nerves were jangled and my heart tender, the day being what it was. But baptizing Heather that day was something other entirely—I can't bear to not capitalize that. It was something Other.

It was my last opportunity to perform one of the sacraments I most held dear, to wash my hands in the holiness of God's sons and daughters. Heaven was skidding into the ground, and the people just kept coming and coming.

By the time I finally got done baptizing people at the second service, I looked to my right at Teddy Hart, my friend and staff pastor. He had been with me since year one, transitioning from a life of more or less biding his time in Cleveland, Tennessee, to becoming an extraordinary preacher, pastor, and friend. A sensitive soul, Teddy's eyes were already red from all the tears he had shed that morning.

"Teddy . . . do we have time for one more?"

Since it was Easter, I was wearing a suit and tie. I did not bother to change; I only took off my shoes. And I joined my people in the abyss. I loved them, and I didn't want to miss my one and only remaining opportunity to jump into the pool with them. I didn't have anybody else to baptize. My last official act as a pastor was already done. I was going to the pool, not as anybody's priest, but as one of them.

The water was cold. My heart was hot. Baptism has a celebratory aspect, but I had no delusions that those moments were anything less than my own funeral. I did not yet know what kind of man I would become when I got out of the water. I had no idea what my life would become. Like the lame man at the pool of Bethesda in the gospels, I only knew angels had been in this water, and I wanted my broken-down body in the pool, in the wake of them.

The life I had built was over. Everything I had been, I was no longer. I had no sense that the water of baptism would magic me into something more, like Clark Kent-suddenly-turned-Superman. But could the water make me, somehow, more human? I wanted to go to the pool because I wanted to embrace my full humanity in the company of my friends, vaguely aware that becoming more human is to have the image of God in us renewed.

Teddy held his hand over my nose. I felt his tears on my head. He could barely get out the words: "Pastor . . . I baptize you in the name of the Father, the Son, and the Holy Spirit." I took the plunge. When I came up, I clutched him like a life preserver. I heard my friends weeping all around me. We all knew this was good-bye.

When There Is No Going Back to the Life You Had Before

Driven by God-knows-what kind of cocktail of nature and nurture, you build the ship you think you always wanted, board by board, or perhaps the ship someone else told you you ought to want. There's relatively little time to think about such things during the massive ego-building project that comprises much of our lives. You rarely even search your pockets anymore to try to find your misplaced reasons. Because there is another paper due, because there is another diaper to change, because there is another plane to catch, because there is another function Friday night that you simply cannot miss. And so you keep on hammering those boards, because somebody has to hammer them; you do what you do, because it's the only thing you know how to do; you keep going where you've always gone, because it's the only way you know to go.

There is nothing particularly bad about the life you've built for yourself—except you're not entirely sure if it's your life you're building, or why you're building a life at all. The world you inhabit is a long way from perfect, but it is mostly ordered. The machines are purring along; the gears are (mostly) working; the soft rhythm of established routine is just enough white noise to drown out the sound of your soul's longing, enough to help you get to sleep at night. So you can get up the next day and start it all over again, without stopping to ask why.

Until the day comes when your ship hits the rocks and you wake up to the violent sound of the sea pouring in through a hole in you. The world outside floods the insulated life you have inside, and the life you knew is now under water. Sometimes the storm crawls in slow and stealthy, catlike, until the first leak springs; sometimes the storm comes sudden, and a rushing mighty wind fills your house like some unholy ghost. It may be that the storm came outside of you and blew in the little sheet of paper on which the doctor wrote the diagnosis; or the tides dragged out the man or woman who said they'd love you forever; or you felt the air grow heavy with electric heat in the air between you on the phone when she said you lost the job. It may also well be it was you who steered straight into the rocks the ship that had kept you more or less afloat all these years—that you now hold yourself responsible for sabotaging the life you told yourself you wanted.

But it does not really matter how you got here or why; and it doesn't really matter if it was God or the devil or yourself or some ancient chaos that spilled up from the bottom of the sea.

What matters now is that you are drowning, and the world you loved before is not your world any longer. The questions of why and how are less pressing than the reality that is your lungs filling with water now. Philosophy and theology won't help you much here, because what you believe existentially about storms or oceans or drowning won't make you stop drowning. Religion won't do you much good down here, because beliefs can't keep you warm when you're twenty thousand leagues beneath the sea.

There is nothing you can find in a book, including this one, that can overwhelm the hard truth you know in the five senses that will not deceive you. You see the unending blackness of a cold sea in front of you. You hear the sound of the bow—and of your own heart—snapping. You taste reality in the salt water burning in the back of your throat. You feel your blood turning to ice under the canopy of the long, arctic night.

The truth is something you already know deep in your own bones: Your ship is sinking. The life you lived before is the life you live no longer; the world you knew before is underwater now. Your life feels like a funeral, because there is a part of you that is actually dying. There are things you are losing now that you won't get back. There is a boy in you who may well be dying for you to become the man you must become now; there is a girl likely breathing her last so a more primal woman may rise to take her place.

The shipwreck is upon you. And there is no going back to the life you had.

The waters that drown are the waters that save.

Before there was a human, there was a

There is a boy in you who may well be dying for you to become the man you must become now; there is a girl likely breathing her last so a more primal woman may rise to take her place.

sea; there was a watery, shapeless chaos, a blackness that had no form and no meaning. Spirit came and hovered over the black, liquid night of the waters; the dove brooded over the anarchy we call sea. And she stayed there long enough, breathed into her deep enough, for life to come up shimmering out of the ocean. It is these primordial waters that we come from, the same water that poured out of the woman you called mother in the hours before you were born. It is into these dark waters that you must return, into this primitive abyss, into this watery grave. You must return again to the chaos of the world you knew before you started trying to build a world you could control—back to the bottom of the ocean where you once lay, submerged.

In secular terms, we call this phenomenon

"drowning"; in the Christian tradition, we call it "baptism."

The bad news is that this shipwreck feels like death, because you really may be dying. The bad news is that old and familiar things you loved and that made you what you were are slowly passing away. The good news is you're being born, and this drowning makes possible the moment when all things become new—most of all, you.

Maybe a preacher on the radio told you once you could be born again if you just repeated a prayer after him. How I wish this were so. But the Scripture where a man named Nicodemus comes under cloak of night for a secret rendezvous with Jesus, and the prophet speaks to him about being born again, is also the place where Jesus talks about that Spirit, the one who broods over the sea, bringing life and beauty out of chaos. The Spirit is like the wind, he says; you don't know where it comes from—and you don't know where it is going. And the people who say yes to this undomesticated Spirit, the people who say yes to the wind—yes to the sea—will be like this Spirit, not knowing where they came from, or where they are going. They are people who learn to trust the wind instead of fighting it, people who learn to navigate the chaos rather than eliminate it. They will be people born of

Spirit, people born of the violence of the storm and the wildness of the wind. And because the Spirit who enters them is the Spirit of life itself, they will live forever.

You can't descend back into the waters of your mother's womb, the prophet tells Nicodemus. But you can be born again; you can be made new. It's just that when you do, it won't be because you made "a decision for Jesus," because you prayed the magic prayer. If you wish to become someone and something else entirely than the you that was before the storm came . . . you will have to peer into the sea that threatens to swallow you whole, dive into the mouth of it—and trust. You will have to let God happen to you, which requires letting life happen to you, all the way down. You cannot continue to flail your arms, beat against the sea, and damn the waves. You have to let yourself go all the way under—into the depths of God, into the depths of your own soul, into the depths, of life itself.

You will have to linger at the ocean floor, where the sea monsters live, and confront everything in you that you've constructed a whole life out of avoiding. You will have to confront the mysteries that lie in the bottom of you. Just in case you are, in fact, drowning and don't feel like you can quite hold out for another hundred pages or more, I'll give you one spoiler: Love is the mystery at the bottom of all the others. To almost everyone's surprise, until an invisible hand holds them underwater long enough, the most beautiful things in all of creation are down here—below, beneath, under the world you knew.

These very waters that are now drowning you have the life-giving power of Spirit within them, deep beneath the current. The waters that drag you down where you do not wish to go—if you do not resist them—will spit you out like Jonah, spewed out of the belly of the whale. And you will burst out of the waters the second time, just like you did the first—screaming in terror; shimmering in your sea-soaked, new skin; glad to be out; terrified to be here . . . yet so wonderfully alive and breathing and so terribly hopeful, no longer encumbered by the things that once dragged you down.

> The Spirit whispers into the pitch-black that surrounds you, carrying the words Jesus spoke to Nicodemus in the wind: You must be born again.

The waters that drown you are the same waters that will save you; and the same sea that is pulling you under is the sea that will make you new. The things you've been holding on to cannot keep you afloat any longer. There is no going back down the birth canal when the Spirit of life is pushing you forward, despite yourself. The only way to lose yourself forever is to keep hanging on to the life you had before. The storm rides you hard, but the Spirit whispers into the pitch-black that surrounds you, carrying the words Jesus spoke to Nicodemus in the wind:

You must be born again.

Holy Ghost Stories

Letting the storm and the night have their way with you, letting the Spirit come in with the wind to make you into something new, is much easier said than done. There are so many reasons not to be reborn. There are so many reasons to choose resuscitation over resurrection. There is nothing quite so scary as the Holy Ghost, because we intuitively know that to make room for this Spirit is to make room for our own upending. Rather than give ourselves over to the whims of that Ghost, it seems at first easier to choose to live as ghosts ourselves. After my own shipwreck, I tried my hand at this for a while.

It was a cold Friday night in my hometown of Charlotte, North Carolina, when I went to the neighborhood bar with my friends who used to work at the church I had founded nine years before. They were still my friends, but I was not their pastor anymore, or anyone of consequence, or anyone—so it felt—in particular. I was on the long side of my own shipwreck, no longer what I was, but altogether unclear on what it was I was becoming. I remember how much I enjoyed the familiar comfort of my friends that night, our easy conversation, and our deep belly laughs. I remember it being one of the rare moments when I enjoyed not being a pastor, enjoyed not doing my best Jesus of Nazareth impression. I liked being a real boy for a few minutes—in a neighborhood bar with friends who stood by me.

That was until my friend Blake told me she saw a girl who used to go to our church playing pool on the other side of the room. The girl, Sarah, was an artist in our town, a friend I had lost track of. But her hair was different, and I told Blake this was not the same girl—which gave way to a bet of sorts and ended with Blake going over to talk to her. And yes, it was the same girl, who had also been glancing over her shoulder our way, trying to figure out if this was her former pastor here in the bar.

So she came over to say hello. I remember feeling a little self-conscious, holding the drink in my hand. For the sake of my mother, I am inclined to want to say I was drinking a Coke—which does have the benefit of being exactly one-half true! So when Sarah came over breezily, I felt myself stiffen just a little. After all, I had baptized her.

All those days for me were marked by the tension of clinging to my old life, a way of wearing a child's floaties in the raging sea and telling myself I was not drowning. I was becoming more and more aware that the life I was living was a half-life, at best.

I used to have a stable marriage, lead a thriving church, and have what felt like an infinite number of friends.

But all that had changed.

In six separate conversations in the three days prior to going to the bar that night, I told people close to me the exact same thing—that the closest thing to a job I had today was being the former pastor of the church I founded and led. I said I felt like the ghost of who I used to be—the pastor of Renovatus.

I used to be the pastor of a thriving church my wife and I planted—a church for liars, dreamers, and misfits. I used to lead this community that was all about love and people and beauty and justice. I used to have a strong marriage to a wife I both admired and adored. I used to be a rising star in my native denomination where my father and grandfather had been pastors. My dad, semiretired, lived ten minutes away and had an office at the church as our volunteer missions pastor. I was living the dream.

I had lived a life that did not deviate from the script I was handed. I loved people the best I knew how. For whatever other shortcomings I had, I had sincerity for days. At our church, we had not built a Christian Walmart; we built counterculture. It was all about the ideas and the people and doing what we did for the sheer love of a thing. Once, while on a mission trip to a Palestinian school we supported, some kids were pointing at me, laughing and saying, "He looks just like Jesus from the video!" I hoped I lived like him too.

But I was not that person anymore.

I had failed in my marriage. I had failed my church. I had failed my friends. I sailed my own ship into the rocks—and both the relationships that mattered most to me and my calling to the church I loved were the casualties.

At thirty-six years old, I was living at my parents' house, ghostwriting for other Christian leaders on my laptop on a folding card table in the utility building where my dad kept his train set. Awash with self-loathing and grief, I was on a descent, and I knew it full well. Only occasionally did I come up for air, to haunt my hometown as a shadow of the man I used to know. Everyone else around me seemed alive enough, and even moving on with their lives, except for me—I was in a cover band, wearing my old clothes, playing the greatest hits of a man who had long since departed.

I was shipwrecked.

I could not go back to the life I had before, but felt incapable of stepping into a new one. I thought often of the verse where Jesus said he saw Satan fall like lightning.[2] But our human falling isn't usually like that—quickly. Most of us fall slowly, hitting every step on the way down—or at least that's what I was doing. Unable to sort out the complicated emotional tangle of my most primal relationships, I had taken myself out of ministry to the people I loved, unresolved, and was wandering around, the ghost of my former self, trying to figure out what to do next.

So this is the space I'm occupying while I chat it up with Sarah, catching up broadly about our lives. I thought it was pleasant enough, but Sarah gave me odd looks, like she could not figure me out somehow, while I was perfectly polite, in my perfectly pastorally trained way. At one point, she laughed, and I asked her why she was laughing, "I don't know, Jonathan. You just . . . still seemed like 'Pastor Jonathan' when you walked in here tonight." I didn't exactly know what to make of this, but a few minutes later, she ambled back over to finish a game of pool with her friends, and I went back to talking with mine.

Until just before I was getting ready to leave, when she came back over a second time and asked if she could talk to me once more. So I waved my friends on and sat down next to her on a barstool. I remembered Sarah as being an intuitive person, as someone who I would have said "walked in the Spirit." And this time when she talked, there was a kind of intensity in her eyes, the wild look I saw on the faces of traveling evangelists as I grew up in rural Pentecostal churches in the South—the look that said the Holy Ghost had taken over.

She said, "Jonathan, I feel like I need to tell you something, but I don't want to offend you. When you walked in here tonight, I was really happy to see you. I was really excited to come over and talk to you and just find out how you're doing and what you're up to these days. But I wasn't excited by the time I walked away from you. I don't know how to put it—you know I think you are a brilliant writer, and your preaching has made such a huge impact on my life. I don't know exactly where you are now or what all you are feeling. But it's like wherever you are right now—you don't know how to really be here. Like you don't know how to own being in a broken place. It's like you still feel the need to put on, like you are the pastor of the church. I think there is so much in you to say and to write that only you can say and write. But it's all going to be a blazing sham if it doesn't come from a truthful place—if it doesn't come from the place you are right here, right now. It's like you don't know how to be comfortable in your own skin. If you like being here in the bar with your friends, that's okay—but be here, be wherever you are now."

Sarah would interrupt herself over and over, apologizing for being so forward, which I waved off. I can recognize the voice of the Spirit, just as much in a bar, and I was entirely open to all that was said. I was hungry to feel seen and known by God, somehow, in my one-foot-in-the-grave, in-between life. It was exactly the feeling I had been describing to my friends. I felt like Bruce Willis at the end of *The Sixth Sense*—that all these things were happening to me and around me; I just didn't know I was the one already dead.

Toward the end, Sarah looked off for a second, pensively, before staring back at me again with the eyes of a prophetess, whatever Spirit had emboldened her: "The best way I'd know how to say it, Jonathan—and I don't want to hurt your feelings!—is that when you walked in the door here tonight, it's like it wasn't Jonathan Martin who walked in the door; it was the ghost of the pastor of Renovatus."

Had I ever heard God speak to me quite so clearly? No wonder when I walked into the bar, Sarah thought she saw a ghost. I was hovering between two worlds, tethered to neither.

Your Faith Will Not Fail, Even When You Do

During that storied final meal Jesus shared with his disciples, only hours away from all the torments that awaited him, there is an extraordinary exchange between Jesus and Peter. The truly remarkable thing is that this is just before Jesus tells Peter he will disown him. Sitting at the table, where the peculiar alchemy of wine turning to blood and bread becoming body was already at play, Jesus looks across the table at the fiery, well-intentioned disciple whose face was not yet shadowed by the guilt of betrayal. And he speaks words of heartbreaking tenderness to the man who says he will die for Jesus but will in actuality curse him by morning: "Simon, Simon, listen! Satan has demanded to sift all of you like wheat, but I have prayed for you that your own faith may not fail; and you, when once you have turned back, strengthen your brothers."[3]

Satan has desired to sift you like wheat, says the man who Roman soldiers will carve up like cattle in just a few hours. But even knowing the physical and psychological torture that he will soon endure, Jesus' concern is for Peter—that he will not be able to live with himself after what he is about to do. He knows the storm of bitter tears, the stomach-churning agony of regret that will eat him from the inside for betraying the one he loved the most. He knows the sting of it could rend Peter's mind, the way the whip will soon rend his own skin. So he says, "I have prayed for you—that your faith may not fail."

Objectively, conclusively, decisively—Peter himself will fail before the rooster crows. That is already established. But while Peter will fail spectacularly, on the surface of things, there is something at work in him that is deeper than his failure. The waves will overtake the man and his blustering ego, but in the depths of the sea within Peter is a stronger, more ancient current that did not originate from him—a current that need not be shaken by his failure on the surface: his faith. I have prayed for you, Peter, that even though you will fail (in fact, be known for the most famous failure in the history of the church), your faith will not fail. The tsunami will come, and take your self-reliance and your pride; humiliation will wash over you. You will fail, but I have prayed for you . . . that your failure would not destroy your faith but deepen it. I have prayed for you that the very thing that was intended to kill you will make the faith already planted in the deepest soil of you even stronger.

It is possible to fail, and not have our faith fail us. It is possible to lose our lives, and not lose our souls. The master teacher taught us himself that it is only in losing our lives—in their ego pretensions and posturing, in their careful image constructions and neediness—that this richer, deeper, below-the-surface life can be found. This is the life hidden with Christ in God, where almost anything can happen at the top of things without disrupting the grace that lies in the bottom of the sea in you. This is the place in the depths where you can be cut off from your very self (as you understood it), and from the name your father gave you, and from the place where you grew up, and from the tribe that gave you language, and from the story that gave you meaning—only to find that nothing can separate you from the love of God.

When the storm is still brewing over the waters, and the sky sickens into an ominous gray-black, and you feel the electric charge in the air in your very skin, inevitably the question comes: Will I survive this? Can I make it through the storm that is coming (whatever sent it here, and however it came)? And of course, there are many storms fierce enough to toss you, throw you, destabilize you, and scare you that do not result in shipwreck.

Some storms last only for the night; some pockets of violent air are only turbulence.

But some storms are more violent, more relentless, more exact-

It is possible to fail, and not have our faith fail us. It is possible to lose our lives, and not lose our souls.

ing. Some winds will not be calmed; some floods will not be dammed until they have their way with you, until they walk away with their pound of flesh. And whether or not, again, the storm finds its origin in the undomesticated wildness of nature and of created things—or whether or not the storm originates in you— does not change the scope or scale or power of it. The storms that come will test us all, and it is entirely possible one comes to you that will end in your failure before the wind and waves recede. But the Spirit in the wind whispers the words of Jesus again, inserting your own name for Simon's: "I have prayed for you that your own faith may not fail—and even when you do . . . that your faith may even grow stronger through your failure."

During my own shipwreck, my long season of descent, I returned over and over to the story in Acts 27 of Paul's shipwreck. The apostle was a prisoner in transport when God revealed to him that a storm was coming. Because Paul knows the Spirit, he is a man in tune with matters of wind and wave as much as the matters of the soul; and he knows the boat he is traveling on will soon encounter a terrible storm. Before the storm comes, he tells his captor companions a heartening thing: "None of you will lose a hair from your heads."⁴ The good news is, you are not going to die. The bad news is, the boat that has been carrying you—the vessel that had taken you from port to port, place to place, the strong and stable boat that made you feel safe on all the oceans you've sailed thus far—the boat will be lost. They were not going to lose their lives, but they were going to lose the boat.

Losing the boat is no small thing. To lose the boat is to lose the ground beneath your feet, the stories you told yourself and others, to lose what protected you from all the elements before. To lose the boat is to lose everything that kept you afloat before, to be thrown into the vast and merciless sea now alone, with nothing left to protect you from its moody tides, the blazing sun above it, or the black-eyed creatures that lurk beneath it. You can lose your boat, lose your house with all the pictures inside it, lose your job, lose your most defining relationship.

And still not lose you.

And still not lose your soul.

And still not lose your faith.

Make no mistake: You will be stripped down in the shipwreck. But you will not be lost.

While I would not recommend a shipwreck to anyone, any more than I would recommend cancer, car accidents, or the plague, I can yet attest to a mysterious truth I have since heard over and over from people who have survived their own shipwrecks: On the other side of them, there is a stronger, deeper, richer, more integrated life. That on the other side of the storm that tears you to pieces is a capacity to love without doubt, to live without fear, to be something infinitely more powerful than the man or woman you were before it happened. Almost nobody who survives a shipwreck would ever sign up to do it all over again, a second time. Nobody can exactly say they were glad it happened. And yet repeatedly, I hear people say the same remarkable thing—that they also under no circumstances would choose to go back and be the person they were before. Nobody would choose to lose the loved one all over again to the unexpected illness, or lose the job they trained for years to get, or lose the relationship they invested heart and soul into for half of their adult life.

I cannot tell you with any degree of confidence that you will not fail your test. I cannot tell you with any degree of certainty that your ship is going to make it out in one piece. Like Job, I am a small man, unable to sort the elements of God and cosmos and good and evil, of human freedom and responsibility, of divine will, or of the unadorned chaos that is the sea itself.

I can only align myself with the greater wisdom of the Teacher and of his apostle and tell you that even though you might fail—utterly— your faith does not have to. I can tell you that even if the ship does not survive, you will.

Storms come, as do a legion of demons that come for the sifting. Take heart; Jesus says, "I have prayed for you."

Chapter Three

Hold On, Let Go

*To let go is to lose your foothold
temporarily. Not to let go is to lose your
foothold forever.*

Søren Kierkegaard

Even as I hold you, I am letting you go.

Alice Walker

There is a small story late in the book of
Acts where the apostle Paul finds himself
shipwrecked. It feels like a bit of a minor entry
in the broad story of the New Testament canon,
not the sort of tale that gets a lot of emphasis
in preaching or Sunday school. But it felt like
there was some treasure hidden in it I needed
to discover somehow. I remember scouring the
passage over and over, trying to find something
to hold on to.

On one level, I knew my shipwreck was
very different from Paul's. It was not his decision to be on a boat to begin with—he had

31

been imprisoned by the Roman government for preaching the gospel and was being transported to another town, still awaiting trial. He was a man subject to the elements and to his enemies, whereas I felt utterly responsible for sailing my ship into the rocks. And yet I also feel a storm is a storm, and a shipwreck is a shipwreck. The main thing I remembered about that story was that Paul and his companions survived, and that was the only thing I knew how to be interested in at that point in my life.

It all started for Paul when a moderate south wind began to blow as the men were about to sail past Crete. But then a violent wind came from the north, crashing down on them from Crete, and the ship could not be turned directly into the wind. So they lost control of the vessel. The storm pounded the ship mercilessly for days. They threw the cargo over, but the storm kept pounding. On the third day, they threw the ship's tackle overboard, but the dark rhythm of the storm did not relent. In a haunting phrase, "When neither sun nor stars appeared for many days, and no small tempest raged, all hope of our being saved was at last abandoned."[1]

And that was where I was. I had tried all the standard maneuvers in the manual—praying, reading, trying to find a friend or therapist who might have a magic word for me. But the storm in me got worse instead of better. I tried to throw some cargo overboard, make minor concessions to the storm, throw out a few things I didn't want anyway. But the storm did not relent. I saw no sun or stars for many days. Swallowed under the canopy of night, neither light nor land was in sight, and I could not shake the feeling in the pit of my stomach that the ship was going to go down, with or without me. In the violence of the storm, there were so many times when I just knew things could not get any worse—and yet the pounding did not stop.

The storm around and within me over-whelmed my senses, but at that point in my life, I simply could not conceive of life without my ship. I would find out later that the ship is not everything—but it sure felt like it was. You can't really overstate the importance of the ship. The ship is the thing that keeps you afloat, that moves you from one place to the next. The ship is the ground beneath your feet that is firm and secure—everything in your life that is known, familiar—no matter how choppy the waves get beneath you. However you got to wherever you are now, there is a ship that got you there.

And precisely because you have weathered many storms in it, the ship means everything to you. In many ways, it feels like the ship is every-thing. There was no way I could have become

the person I was then, or am now, apart from
my marriage and my vocation as pastor of the
church I planted. It's understandable, then, how
easy it is to make the move from "the ship feels
like everything to me" to "the ship is everything
to me." The ship on which you ate and drank,
laughed and cried, sailed and struggled, is so
connected to you that it feels like it is you. That
you would not know how to be, or if you could
be, in the world without it.

The men on Paul's ship were out of food and
had lost heart. But that is when the weathered
apostle gives them some good news: The angel
of God had appeared to him and told him not to
be afraid. The angel said Paul was going to survive the storm, and so would everyone traveling
with him. Some sailors were about to escape,
but Paul tells them if they don't all stay on the
boat, they won't be saved. They were going to
have to stick around long enough to endure the
horrors yet to come. They were going to have to
be fully present and accounted for, for the loss of
the ship. They would have to feel it, experience
it—the dreaded fear of the soul-black night and
raging storm—until the bitter end. They would
not lose their lives, but they would have to lose
their ship.

And yet the old vessel was not wasted. The
structure that carried them from the port would

carry them no longer. The ship would not survive as a coherent vessel; it would be torn to shreds. But then there is this crucial detail: When the ship sinks, the men grab planks, boards, tiny remaining fragments of the ship—and those small pieces of the wreckage carry them safely to the shore.

When you are in a shipwreck, the first response is always to grasp desperately for someone or something to hold. It is not calculated, but instinctive—a mad, almost flailing attempt to find something to grip. There may be little left to cling to, but there has to be at least some kind of holding on—even if it is just a tacit agreement within yourself to simply keep on living. In this case, holding on is not a metaphor or an abstraction; it is a way of finding a reason, however strong or flimsy it might be, to survive.

Something inside you wants this, even when you otherwise are altogether uncertain as to whether or not you consciously want to survive. That part of you that kicks and screams to still be here is your soul. The soul does not make a home, on the surface of things, so it has largely stayed out of sight, almost in hiding, the bowed head and quiet eyes of a nun in a convent. You can cover up the soul under layers of duty and obligation—you can muzzle it—making only an occasional appearance in moments of joy or of ecstasy before slinking back into the bottom of you, sleeping through its days—a creature of the shadows.

Until the shipwreck, when the soul reasserts itself. You know it is there, because you can hear it scream and because you can feel it bleed. You almost didn't notice it at all, until you heard the sound of what seemed like your soul, dying. And yet precisely because the soul bears the finger-prints of the Spirit, it does not need any reasons to go on—it was no creature of reason to begin with. It needs no logic to fight back; it needs no will in order to survive. When everything else in and around you is dead or dying, the soul will not yet go quietly. Your soul is not dead yet, just because it decided not to be; it claws its way back up through all the grief, without your consent, like some kind of animal.

You're Still Here

The first things overboard when your ship wrecked were all the reasons you ever had for sailing. And when the life you knew is a life you know no longer, and the ship that took you on a thousand adventures before can no longer even keep you afloat, you are right to wonder if there is anything left worth having.

There used to be so many things that we could not live without! How could you live without this person? How could you live without this job? How could you live without this relationship? How could you live without this house? How could you live without your dignity? How could you live without your good reputation? And then death came to someone you loved, or you lost the job, or you sabotaged the relationship or felt your love sabotaged you, or you suffered public humiliation, or you lost your all-important sense of honor. And you thought you really would die.

There was a part of you, maybe even a really large part of you, that really did. There are some losses that in their way mark you forever, and some things you never get over. And because you loved this person or this life and career you built, or valued your dignity, when the bow broke, everything in you screamed. While the sails were ripping and the boards splitting, you heard the sound of your spirit dying. The life you had was over. But to your own shame, *you* were not over, as much as you may have wanted to be. Maybe like a proud samurai, it seemed the best thing you could do on the other side of the shipwreck was to fall on your own sword and stage a protest against anything you once found beautiful. Because you were so sad. Because you were so guilty. Because you were so scared that in the loss of something outside yourself, you lost your own heart to the sea's black rage.

And then came what might be the worst discovery: You didn't die—not really. You walked away from the accident, whether or not you think you or God or the devil or the fates are somehow responsible for it. You just knew you would die, and at times it felt like something in you did. But not *you*. Not all of you, anyway. The ship may have gone down, but miracle of miracles, you're still here.

Can you remember the first time after the funeral, after you could not bear to eat or drink, that the pangs of hunger overwhelmed you? Did you feel incredulous at yourself, at the animal part of you that still wanted food after such a thing? What about when there was a particular taste you wanted, because it was a taste that on some level you actually desired? However much fog, however much sorrow, however much grief—the experience of loss may have altered your taste buds forever. But it hardly killed them.

You watched dreams you cradled in your arms with the strength of all your tenderness descend into the sea. All that animated you, all that moved you before, could move you forward in the world no longer. The water filled your mouth and your nostrils, and you choked at the taste of it. But when the grief or the guilt or the loss recedes into the night and your soul sets sail again, you still dream—despite yourself. There is still a kind of music you will hear that stirs within you an unspeakable longing. There is still an ache, not just for all you lost, but to see and know and be seen and known still, to explore and imagine and create. However much the longing for the past may assault your senses, it is not the only longing that remains. There is still a part of you that wants to make love, to feel yourself somehow connected. There is still a part of you that yearns for something outside yourself. You felt yourself out to sea, and yet some kind of desire, for something or another, bears you along, and you find yourself still somehow here—almost against your own wishes. And even in the moments when anything that felt like conscious desire went out with the tide, there is still some kind of near-morbid curiosity of how your life and story are going to turn out—even if you are lost enough to only behold what's left of your life as a kind of bystander.

Somewhere between your body's animal refusal to go down quietly, your mind's refusal to stop imagining, and your heart's refusal to stop dreaming, in the tangled mess of synapses and memories and impulses, there lies God. In whatever remains in you that wants to create, to make, to birth something new, in whatever corner that longs for some kind of resurrection on the other side of death, something divine quietly snaps, fires, clicks, flickers. This is the Spirit of God, lurking in your own broken spirit.

You may find that your grief and sense of loss over the world you once knew seem endless. And yet there are possibilities and potentialities within you that are more endless still. What is this unseen force that carries you forward despite yourself? Why can you not seem to choke, always and forever, your own irrational yearning, this buried but still breathing hope for more?

This ache is God's fingerprint. The stirring to create, to love, to live, to give of yourself when there is no self left to give—this comes from the Spirit. You were created in the image of God. Before you knew anyone or did anything, everything was in you necessary to live at home in divine love. However buried that image of God is within you, that part of you that knows what it is to be perfectly loved, held, and known—it is still very much there. There is a part of you that does not need anything else, or anyone else in particular, to be alive. There is a part of you that knows this—part of you that has *always* known this—but has long since forgotten.

The God who sustains all created things

with love sustains you. The God who created the world not to be exploited, dominated, or needed, but to love and to enjoy without clinging, is awake in your belly. And so in you is the capacity to love and to live without needing the world to work out a certain way in order for you to be okay. Your life, your existence, is contingent on that Spirit. But it is not contingent on anyone else, or anything else.

> This ache is God's fingerprint. The stirring to create, to love, to live, to give of yourself when there is no self left to give—this comes from the Spirit.

This is the liberating, terrifying discovery of life on the other side of the shipwreck. That while you are a creature—humble, dependent, small, in need of love and food and shelter— you didn't need anything else as much as you thought you did. That the things you knew would kill you don't actually kill you. That the fire in you the sea should have drowned out, burns within you yet, if you do not let yourself smother it (and maybe even if you do). So much of the world you have known is no more. But if there is any truth in any of this at all, the shipwreck that threatened to destroy you utterly may be the thing that saves you yet. It may not drown you; it may transfigure you.

And if there is something truthful, something larger, about this irrational lust for life that is forged in the fires of death, it says something too about the people you lost. For if there is a God who not only creates but sustains and resurrects, then there can yet be life on the other side of death for all things. Then there is hope, not only for the yearning in you to drive you into union with God, but to be realized in union with those others. If death is not the final word, and chaos produces creation rather than destroys it, then many of the stories of the life you thought were long over are far from over yet.

Believing this won't mean you won't still feel the weight of deep, sharp, piercing grief, or that you should feel guilty when you do. On the contrary, people who don't experience deep pain have not experienced deep love and are not to be envied. That doesn't mean they are shallow—all of our souls surely have something of the same depths—they just may not be aware of their own yet. That day will come for them. But when you feel your own deep capacity for passion, compassion, mourning, even rage, you are glimpsing something of your soul's own infinite capacity to know, to feel, and to become. Within the depths of all you feel the most deeply, something of the Spirit's own immortal depths is reflected in you. We have a capacity for love and hope and beauty seemingly too big for our heads and hearts, because we are created in the image of God.

Cling to Nothing . . . but Hold On

After the shipwreck, when the ship is still going down and all you have left are bits of it still floating in the sea all around you, it's nearly impossible to tell at first what will actually hold you up. The ground that was once beneath your feet is now scattered all around you; and you know instinctively that much of what has gone before, you can't take with you now.

So the attempt to find something to hold you up is often a very high-stakes kind of trial and error. Some of what was holding you up was built on lies, spin, and youthful delusions. You must let them float away. Some of the childish notions of how the world works—the illusion that you were ever truly in control of your life to begin with—you must let sink. Some of them made for a helpful enough vessel at the time, getting you from point *a* to point *b*, moving you forward. Some of the relationships that cannot and probably should not survive the storm served an invaluable function for a while. But the shipwreck has made new demands of your life, and much of what carried you before cannot carry you now—and you surely aren't in a position to carry much of anything with you now.

After the shipwreck, you may have little left to hold on to. And yet you must find a reason to hold on. This is much more difficult than it sounds, because surviving the shipwreck, in general, has much more to do with letting go than it does with holding on. You are now trying to simultaneously find a way to hold on while learning to live with open hands and an open heart—to not resist the wind, or the Spirit you find in it.

Growing up in Pentecostal churches, I spent a lot of my childhood attempting to chase down the Holy Ghost. The preacher would give an invitation for people to be filled with the Spirit—which we would know occurred when we let go of the ordered world of rational speech and God moved on us to talk with unknown tongues. Even where I parse some of these things differently now, there is still a way it makes some kind of soulish sense to me. Aren't we all, in some way or another, looking for an experience that will transcend the pale and paltry words we know? Isn't there something inside all of us that wants to howl, that wants to rumble, that wants to talk in unknown tongues? The letting go of mind and of ego, the sense of being acted upon by something larger, older, truer—surely there is something of this that the soul has always wanted, whether we can acknowledge it in our minds or with our words at all.

I remember going down to the altar, wanting the gift of the Spirit, but being confounded by the sweet old saints who tried to help me "pray through." I would be down at the front of the church, my eyes squeezed tightly shut and my hands raised like awkward lightning rods, praying to receive the power. And I'd have some dear old sister in one ear, shouting, *Hold on, brother!* And there would be some dear old sister in the other ear who would shout, *Let go, brother!* That is the Pentecostal version of paradox. I wasn't ready to explore many others, but that was one I got baptized into early. How is it possible to hold on and let go at the same time? I don't know that I can even answer that question now, but I do know life with God exists somewhere at that intersection. That somewhere between holding on and letting go is where you are liable to stumble into, or perhaps even collide into, resurrection. The old-time Pentecostals may have been even more right than they knew.

In the shipwreck, you find yourself smack-dab in the middle of having to let go of everything you thought you knew—and yet still trying to find a reason to hold on when you don't feel like you've got anything to hold on to.

One Small Plank

In the shipwreck, you may feel like you lost it all. Everything is in pieces. But in the fragments, there are planks that remain—pieces of desire, of dreams, of hope, of imagination, of longing, that rise to the top of you even now. They are no longer attached neatly together, but they are still afloat in the swirling chaos of you. You may not need all of them. Perhaps you don't need many of them. But you almost certainly need one of them. Wherever and however you feel your soul still adrift, grab hold of one of them. Don't cling too tightly to it; let the weight of it hold you up rather than the other way around. Anything that's survived by now surely has something of Spirit's power in it. It may be a plank that is older than you, a plank that might outlast you.

Grab something—anything—that will help you get through the night. That will help you make it to the shore.

It does not have to be anything big enough or strong enough to hold you up forever. Just something you can reach out for, lean your head against, and rest on when the night falls. Not enough to rebuild a life, but enough to get you to shore. You may think you will not yet survive the waves, but Spirit comes in the wind—to guide your giant soul and your tiny plank to a place called home.

You only need one small plank, one reason not to give up, one reason to stay alive . . . today. At the very least, your life itself is a sign and a sacrament for someone else, a light in someone else's darkness. There is not a thing in the world wrong with staying alive—for now—for their sake more than your own. That was what I found when I went to an Episcopal church in downtown Charlotte after I left the church—and it largely became that small plank for me. The simple liturgy, week after week, did not remove all my pain but gave me a reason to keep going—from one Sunday to the next Sunday, until the next, sustaining me somehow, then, in the days between.

It is always good and right in a time of shipwreck to cling to a community. It is good to cling to friends too, though part of what makes the shipwreck so intense is that by nature it's a time when friendships are largely being renegotiated. And of course, then, it is the best possible time to cling to God.

And yet even that does not come quite without qualification. It would seem this might be the easiest, most universal statement: "Well, at least you can still hold on to Jesus." The trouble with holding on to God is that often we cling to an old idea about God—perhaps one we needed to let go of all along—rather than to God himself.

Holding on to Jesus surely is always the right thing to do—unless you are Mary Magdalene, whom Jesus appears to first just after he rose from the dead. Her world has been eclipsed by the storm. Days before, she watched the man her heart burned for be tortured and killed. Now, the dead man is standing in front of her. Which is more disorienting? What is for certain is that her world is upended. Desperately, instinctively, she lunges for what is familiar—the body of Jesus impossibly standing in front of her now, only a few feet away. "Don't embrace me, Mary. I have not yet ascended to the Father," Jesus says.[2] It is not that Jesus was no longer there for her; it is that Jesus cannot be there for her in the ways he was there for her before. She would have to come to know him in a different way. Resurrection had not yet finished working out its terrible implications. There would be no time to cling to a form of Jesus, an idea of Jesus, a vision of Jesus, she used to have. She would have to know him now on the other side of the trauma that is resurrection, so that even "clinging to Jesus" was

not going to work in
the ways it had worked
already.

You can't even cling
to the God you knew,
*only to the God you can
know now.*

You can't even cling
to the God you
knew, *only to the God
you can know now.*

Let Go

So for Mary, as it is for most of us, the hardest
part is not the holding on but the letting go.
That was the part I really didn't know how to
do. Because I never let go. I kept such a tight
grasp on anything or anyone I claimed to love,
and the more I hurt, the more I dug my finger-
nails into anything that would seem to keep me
alive. I was so afraid of letting go.

One of the main reasons I could not let go
was that I knew I was propping up other people.
If I let go, what would happen to the people
leaning on me? My heart was in tatters, but I
stood there quivering, still clinging to the twin
pillars of duty and obligation. I was not standing
strong, but I was not lying down. When the
storm first broke and I felt like I needed to quit, I
remember the staff member who leaned in three
times within fifteen minutes to say, "You cannot

leave. *Livelihoods* are at stake." I was my father's son, the apple of his eye as a rising star in the denomination. What would my family do? And besides, this was a church I had helped bring into the world. What would the church do? I was trying to say, even though everything in me said my time was over, that the only hope for me was to pull the plug and put real weight down on the hope of resurrection. But I had convinced myself I could not, because too many people and too many things were dependent on me.

It is fascinating to me now to see how, even though I know better, there is something that feels pious and noble about that sentiment. That it sounds like God and gospel to me—to stay in at all costs because it is for someone else's sake. It is hard to hear the whisper of the ego underneath all that, saying, "You are *too important*."

Accepting Our Own Smallness

The primary obstacle to letting go is generally our own inflated opinions of ourselves—that our lives are too important, that too much depends on us . . . that the world cannot go on without us. Part of the function of the ship-wreck is to show us the truth that was there long before the storm came: We are much smaller, and much less important, than we think we are.

While my world was imploding, I went by myself one Wednesday afternoon to see the film *All Is Lost*. I didn't go into a movie theater; I went into a metaphor. Everywhere I turned, there was language and images of sea—symbolic in Hebrew mythology of chaos, of the abyss. I knew no other way to describe the way I felt except lost at sea—adrift and alone. Which is of course precisely what the film is about. In it, seventy-seven-year-old Robert Redford plays a man whose boat is torn open at sea. His communications system is beyond repair.

The weathered Redford is by himself against the elements, a speck of a human against the unending mystery of the sea. There were two shots in that film that sliced through me. In one, the camera pans up slowly from the tiny raft he now occupied and just keeps going up, until the perspective crawls over you of just how small he is against the expanse of ocean. But there is a second shot I loved even more—essentially the same shot, but from the bottom of the raft. The camera descends lower and lower, slowly, until not only do you see the tiny raft from the opposite depth, but you also see a school of sharks swimming beneath him, undetected by the protagonist.

Months later, I was sitting downstairs in a tiny makeshift chapel on the bottom floor of a simple condo in San Diego, California. Across from me in the unadorned sanctuary was Sister Anne, a nun in her late sixties. There were no vestments, no ceremonial attire, just a simple black track jacket. She had a dark, natural tan in the easy way people do in Southern California, her face framed by short, soft white hair and gold-rimmed glasses. Her voice soothed the storm in me. Her eyes, bright and blue and young and curious, peered into the abyss that had swallowed me whole, unflinching. I knew little except there was no judgment in this tiny woman, that love seemed to follow her in like a song. For three days, she had been taking me apart, touching all my pressure points gently—I called her the Ignatian ninja. Each day, she sent me out into the place I most tended to avoid in the indoor sport that was my life—into the wild. Sometimes to the cliffs, sometimes to the pier, sometimes up a mountain. She said I needed to clear space for myself, that I needed to get to places where I could see and feel myself from God's point of view.

Sister Anne was also the extremely cultured nun who apparently sees all the credible new art films. She said to me, "Jonathan, I don't know if you have seen the film *All Is Lost* with Robert

Redford. But it makes me think of you. It is about a man who had read all these books about the sea and had all these wonderful instruments. But it was not until he was an old man caught in a terrible storm that he finally had to learn how to use them for himself."

I could not help but laugh. Sister Anne was right. My knowledge was more theoretical than experiential. This was the season of on-the-job, in-the-storm training of the life-or-death variety. This was the divinity school with no roof, no bottom, no boundaries, and no end in sight.

I was a man out of his depth, dealing with the sea that had always been within me. But I never had the scale and perspective to see either my smallness or the infinite varieties of creatures that dwelled within my own depths. Of course I did not want to look at them.

I was not going to be able to let go as long as I thought the world was going to collapse if I did so. What I did know was that I thought I was going to have a nervous breakdown if I stayed where I was. As bad as I was at listening to my body or integrating it into my spirituality, I could not ignore it this time. So I gathered the pieces of myself that were left to be gathered and headed to that little Catholic retreat center in San Diego on just a few days' notice.

As I followed Sister Anne's instructions each

day to go out into creation, she told me to feel
the energy of the waves and water and wind—to
let the Spirit blow through me and enter me
through them. All week, I kept thinking about
the verse in Acts where Paul says, "In him we live
and move and have our being."[3] I would walk the
cliffs and could not shake the awareness that the
Spirit was actually in the wind. Never before in
my life had I been so aware that when I did look
at the rocks or the waves or the sky, God was
in all of that, was holding all of it. Sometimes I
would stop and lie down on the rocks, and I just
couldn't escape the truth of it: "The Spirit is in
the wind; the Spirit is in the wind; the Spirit is
in the wind." The inescapability of God's love
would not let me go:

> Where can I go from your spirit?
>> Or where can I flee from your presence?
> If I ascend to heaven, you are there;
>> if I make my bed in Sheol, you are there.
> If I take the wings of the morning
>> and settle at the farthest limits of
>>> the sea,
> even there your hand shall lead me,
>> and your right hand shall hold me fast.
> If I say, "Surely the darkness shall cover me,
>> and the light around me become night,"
> even the darkness is not dark to you;

the night is as bright as the day,
for darkness is as light to you.[4]

There is no escape from love. It fills all
things. The Spirit of God—she fills all things.
And I could feel her filling me, fractured and
broken though I was.

It is an illusion-shattering thing to be out-
doors, away from the insulation of rooms and
hard corners, and face fully the essential wildness
of things. In our own kingdoms of influence—
our homes, our pulpits, our offices, our
computers—we fancy ourselves in control, cre-
ators rather than conduits. Climate-controlled
rooms delude us into thinking we can control
God and the world. In reality, the thermostat
is about all we can change. It's impossible to be
people of the Spirit while disconnected from
nature—the creation—where the Spirit's wildness can be learned. I needed to be away from
the technology that says, "You are really *big*!"
Nature says, "Oh honey, you are really, really
small." We poke fun at ancient mythologies we
find absurd while buying the most absurd of
them all—the myth that we control things.

I was getting away from my delusions of
control. I was getting back in touch with my
own breath again. Sister Anne directed me to
slow down my breathing, to breathe deeply, to

let God set my breathing right again. In the evenings, I would go down to the little library at the center and wrap myself in a blanket, and imagine that the blanket was the love of God itself. Sitting in the little rocker, I would let myself be held. I would tell God how afraid I was.

"The conversion moment in us is when we see from a new perspective," Sister Anne said. "Sometimes all we can see is that this is not working for us anymore. That is all you can see, until you are ready to see from that new perspective." Everything she asked me to do that week was about perspective. To walk along the shore and pick up small rocks, allowing them to become stand-ins for all my troubles—and then fling them into the expanse of the ocean. As I did, I grasped their smallness; I heard the small plunk against the backdrop of the roar of the waves.

"God looks at us and sees us the way we see ants," Sister Anne told me one day. "We see them working so hard to build their little structures, and we think it is cute or even admirable. We enjoy their beauty for a moment. But we know the next day, someone will come along and step on their little ant colony, and all they worked so hard to build will be gone."

"God sees us as parents would see a two-year-old child," she continued. "They are sorry when they make a mess, but they are not surprised by it. They hate to see them hurt themselves in some way, but they are not angry at them for it. It is also true that our grandest successes, our biggest accomplishments, are like the drawings of a two-year-old. God delights in them only because he delights in us, but they are no more impressive. He just likes that we drew it. But they are still very small and simple to such a great God," she said. "That's how God sees your work," she added, smiling.

A shipwreck has a way of stripping you bare, of exposing your own finite smallness against the infinite horizon of a dark sea. Slowly but surely, I was being delivered from my own sense of importance. As I now know, it is possible to devote yourself to a life of piety, keep all the rules, and even engage in the spiritual disciplines—but leave the ego largely untouched. We have developed ways we can "be a good Christian" without ever embracing the descent into death and resurrection that would actually turn us into good human beings. I think a lot of this has to do with the project the church often sanctions every bit as much as the rest of the world does—the life of working hard to be a "success." In the words of Thomas Merton, "If I had a message to my contemporaries, I said, it was surely this: Be anything you like, be madmen, drunks, and bastards of every shape and form, but at all costs avoid one thing: success . . . If you are too obsessed with success, you will forget to live. If you have learned only how to be a success, your life has probably been wasted."[5]

The years prior to all this had been my most successful in ministry. And not just successful in the sense of climbing some ladder of temporal gain—it was the most effective preaching and teaching I had ever done. But there was so much of myself I had kept at bay. Sister Anne helped me see I was like the young surgeon she heard lecturing about suffering when she was in medical school (she was a very smart nun)—I knew all about the tools and instruments, but had not known about grief and pain before now, had not had to really wrestle with the mysteries for myself.

I don't think I had deeply come to know love yet either. In recent years, I had repeated revelations of the love of God, whether through Scripture, books, or things I would see in other people. But I had yet to really allow the love of God to settle over me in all my broken places, to come to really know divine love in the parts of me that seemed the most unlovable. My theory is that all of us elder sons of the church, the ones who spend all our lives trying to keep the rules, have a deep suspicion that if we do feel loved and accepted, it is because we are working so hard to get it right. Sister said it takes some people their whole lives to come to really believe God loves them. But that it had to be learned in a deep, experiential way—as it is the key to existence. She said that no matter how long it took, God is relentlessly determined for me to really *know* this for myself. Sister Anne said the whole trauma I was experiencing—of going through hell, of falling apart, of death and resurrection—was for my good, so I could really know.

Per usual, God did not answer any of the questions I went to San Diego asking—questions about ministry and marriage, about what would come next. But I did feel like God spoke to me, again in that way when you feel things inside you shift, and it is as if some new word has been planted in the topsoil of you—small and green and hopeful. I tried to pray a lot that week, often in its most primal forms of letting my very breath become prayer. Mindful, attentive, at peace for the first time in five months, I would stand on the pier at night and watch the waves roll in and out, knowing they were coming in and out long before I got there, and they would continue to long after I was gone. Walking through a graveyard on a mountain, I tasted my smallness in a world where so many people are being born and are dying—and do so with or without me. Looking out over the ocean, I saw my smallness against the horizon.

The search for meaning is a quest for power we are not designed to bear, an obstacle to the grace of insignificance. What could prepare us for the breath of God (Spirit) that hums all life into being, except we be emptied of our pretensions of significance? Divine perspective most of all relativizes our importance. We are each very small creatures. Very little is contingent on us. Knowing our smallness puts us in touch with the essential lightness of created things—transitory, ephemeral creatures. Splendid irrelevance. All lives are small lives; all epic struggles are skirmishes, because we are weightless creations, deceived by an illusory sense of gravity. Inside the movie inside our head, we all feel like we are stars. It's an illusion. We're all extras.

Destinies do not rest on our shoulders. We are given choices, but the cosmos runs with or without us. And that is all grace.

The gospel doesn't fulfill our quest for significance, but exposes its essential folly. It gives us something better than meaning—namely, love. The love of God gives us unfathomable value despite our objective smallness. But it still leaves us blissfully unimportant.

The two central exchanges in my own time with God, as best as I could discern them, went something like this:

Me: "God, I can't take this. I honestly think I'm falling apart."

God: "What would be so wrong with you falling apart?"

Me: "Well . . . I mean, I've got this thing you gave me to do. And I don't think I can do it anymore. I think I'm going to have to go sell french fries at McDonald's."

God: "Who told you you couldn't work at McDonald's?"

I was starting to see. I am a creature: made, dependent, small. I know less than I think I do. I think more rides on my existence than it ever does. I was coming to see that wisdom is not having the right answers but having a proper sense of scale and perspective. Wisdom is embracing our blissful smallness. If we think the world needs us too much, we can't receive life as gift. And if we can't receive life as a gift, we can't receive it at all. The tides keep coming in and out; the flowers keep growing; people keep being born and dying. It all keeps running, not contingent on us.

Destinies do not rest on our shoulders. We are given choices, but the cosmos runs with or without us. And that is all grace.

Chapter Four

Eating, Breathing, Sleeping

*Out of the darkness of my life, so much
frustrated, I put before you the one
great thing to love on earth: the Blessed
Sacrament . . . There you will find
romance, glory, honour, fidelity, and the
true way of all your loves upon earth.*

J. R. R. Tolkien

*Holy Communion is offered to all, as
surely as the living Jesus Christ is for all,
as surely as all of us are not divided in
him, but belong together as brothers and
sisters, all of us poor sinners, all of us
rich through his mercy. Amen.*

Karl Barth

Perhaps the most universal experience in any
and all kinds of shipwrecks is the way they
strip us down to the primary colors of being

human. There are so many things we have, that we come to think we need, that we feel we cannot live without. On the one hand, the prospect of liberation that the shipwreck offers (if we survive it!) is a life where we are set free from that illusory sense of need for things that are not necessary at all. In the shipwreck, we come to find out the list of things we need to stay alive is relatively short—we need to breathe, we need to eat, we need to sleep, we need companionship of some kind. A shipwreck is the most radical act of cleaning out our closets. When we get over the initial terror of it, there is a kind of exhilaration in getting rid of so much we never really needed but thought we could not live without. It is good to not feel ourselves so dependent on things that never really sustained us to begin with. Through the horror of our losses, we slowly gain a clarity, composure, and clearheadedness that was never available to us before the storm.

What makes this so complex, however, is that in the same moment we are finding these essentials are all we really need to survive— breathing, eating, sleeping, friendship—we also find ourselves struggling with these most basic human practices we may have taken for granted before. We did not worry too much about having enough oxygen, until we were plunged into the depths of the sea. We didn't worry too much about dinner, when we knew there would be plenty of money to go out for it. We didn't think too hard about sleeping, before the shipwreck invaded our dreams and disrupted our sleep. We discover we had all the essential things we needed to survive in us and around us all along, while at the exact same time we are discovering these things are now harder to come by than they ever were before.

Whereas the early stages of shipwreck entail a sense of panic, a frantic kind of triage, trying to figure out what we can salvage and what we cannot, eventually we have to slow down . . . and return to those primary colors. In order to not drown, we have to find a way to ground our bodies long enough to figure out how to breathe and sleep and be again, without the comfort and props we had before. It is not easy to do, because nothing is easy to do after the shipwreck. But the gift is a kind of simplicity: I don't have time or strength enough now to wrestle with large existential questions. I cannot fix anybody else's problems. I am not strong enough to be productive in all the ways I was before. I have to stay alive. I have to survive. So I have to figure out a way to do all of these things, again . . . somehow.

The apostle Paul is one of the master

teachers in any and all wisdom traditions, a
man you would want to talk to in order to find
answers to all your questions about finding
meaning in the cosmos. And yet in our Acts
27 story, when Paul receives revelation by the
Spirit that he and his companions were about to
experience a shipwreck, Paul does not give them
philosophical, theological, abstract counsel. All
too often, people of faith like me behave more
like the friends of Job than the friends of Jesus,
lecturing, pontificating, preaching, or explain-
ing suffering—well-intentioned maybe, but
useless in the face of real pain. But the apostle is
wise enough not to say anything smart or clever,
wowing his boat mates with penetrating insights
into the meaning of the sea and the existential
function of the shipwreck. Instead, Paul gives
them astonishingly bald, unadorned, practical
advice that will help keep them alive:

> "For the last fourteen days," he said,
> "you have been in constant suspense
> and have gone without food—you
> haven't eaten anything. Now I urge you
> to take some food. You need it to sur-
> vive. Not one of you will lose a single
> hair from his head." After he said this,
> he took some bread and gave thanks

to God in front of them all. Then he
broke it and began to eat. They were all
encouraged and ate some food themselves. Altogether there were 276 of us
on board. When they had eaten as much
as they wanted, they lightened the ship
by throwing the grain into the sea.[1]

Paul says in effect, "You've worried your-
selves to death, so much so that you haven't
even been able to eat. You'll be okay, but only
if you eat enough so the storm doesn't take too
much out of you when it hits." As it is with
all hungry and hurting people, they didn't
need a philosophy seminar; they needed to be
fed. They didn't need meaning; they needed a
meal. Paul was an expert Jewish teacher, but he
doesn't break down Torah law for the sailors;
he breaks bread for them. He gives thanks;
then he distributes the bread. This fits the pat-
tern of how God responds to human suffering:
We come looking for answers; God sends a hot
meal through a warm body. We come looking
for reasons for our hunger; God sends provision
to feed us. We come looking for a sermon that
will explain the complexity of the cosmos to us
and satiate our desire for understanding; Christ
responds with, "This is my body, given for you;

this is my blood, shed for you."

People try to offer us an explanation; God offers us a Eucharist.

People try to offer us an explanation; God offers us a Eucharist.

Eating

The meal Paul offers may be called "a Eucharist" for a handful of reasons. Eucharist, by definition, is "giving thanks." It's a meal Paul gives thanks for, blesses, and distributes to everyone on board, regardless of tribe or tradition. I presume that Luke, the author of Acts, knows what he is doing in using language and imagery so rich in eucharistic imagery, connecting it with the ritual as established in the earliest Christian communities. And I do believe there is something consecrated, something remarkably other, about this meal in particular, which I'll return to shortly.

But for our purposes here, it's important to put the eucharistic meal in the context of the broader story of God and humanity. At least part of the reason God reveals himself in flesh and blood in Jesus of Nazareth, the incarnate Word made flesh, is to show us that all humans are holy. The gospels place a relentless emphasis on the bodily resurrection of Jesus, because it is through attending to the sacredness of his earthly body that we can learn to recognize the sacredness of all bodies. We recognize sacred spaces and consecrate holy ground, because it is in these places that we can learn to live in the reality that all space is sacred and all ground is holy because God created and sustains it. In the same way, part of the function of the holy meal, the Eucharist, is that through this consecrated supper, we are learning to recognize the essential holiness of all suppers. Even the honor given to the priest or pastor who presides over the meal is teaching us, if we are paying attention, to regard all those who will ever prepare a meal for us as holy chefs. In the consecration of the elements, we see that all who cook and prepare bread and wine for the sake of caring for someone else's body reenact the liturgy. If we are wise, perhaps we may learn to bow to all of them yet.

When we are able to eat on the other side of a shipwreck, all meals are especially holy, because the sea and storm have sapped us of all our former strength. The primal blessing of food, so often taken for granted, is exotic to us again. How is it, anyway, that no matter how much or how badly we have suffered, even when it does entail not wanting to eat for a few days, we still get hungry again, and that against all odds, food tastes good to us still? Isn't it fascinating that even when we are completely out of sorts, there is something about a meal (any meal), that grounds us again in our humanity— especially when it's a meal shared with others?

When you are trying to survive a shipwreck, I am very much in favor of eating. I will not put parameters on this. I am sure that when you are dealing with physical or psychological trauma, there are many benefits to eating clean and healthy so your body can function as well as possible. I would not argue against this. There have been times of shipwreck when a very disciplined diet, the routine of monitoring what I ate when, seemed to have a soothing quality, providing a kind of order and stability in times when the world was all chaos. I would celebrate anything that helps you survive a storm, including embracing the mental and physical sharpness that comes with reducing carbs and sugars—though I love them more than I love you and would choose their survival in the event of apocalypse over your own.

But short of recommending alcoholism or cocaine, I'm a pretty big fan of the whatever-it-takes-to-get-you-through-the-night diet as well. Maybe you shouldn't have cheesecake every night forever, but if you'd look forward to it, be fully present to it, and be grateful for it, let the cheesecake tether you again to what is good about the earth. Let the cheesecake make you believe in God again, and the idea that there must still be something good left on earth because of how good this is tasting right now. Whatever meal would make you feel like giving thanks is provision that syncs you again to the Provider. If it's between eating something you love and hating your life tonight, eat something good—and make no apology for it! And if you need to be healthy to keep your strength up to survive the shipwreck over the long haul, eat the cheesecake tonight, and an apple in the morning—and start over. Now is not the best time to agonize over the calorie count. To eat is to be human, to eat is to celebrate being alive— especially when you eat with other people. If there is a place you can go to be fed a meal, and a person you know with whom you can enjoy a meal, this is no small part of what it takes to survive a shipwreck.

Those small moments of gratitude may be the only thing that keeps you afloat. It is not selfish to do what you have to do to take care of yourself in the wake of all the pain. Nights will come when the taste of food may be the closest thing to feeling anything at all, and that is okay. A hot meal can tether you to reality again, root you down in the provision of God.

For a moment, it can make you feel human, and when there is nothing else you know how to feel grateful for, it may just be reason enough to mutter "thanks" under your breath—and be aware, if even for a moment, this meal means you are not entirely alone.

But there is a special place for the consecrated meal in the season of shipwreck too. I do not come from a tradition where we partook of Communion often, at least in my corner of the tradition. But during my years as a pastor, the power of this practice came alive in my life and the life of our church in such a transformative way. We celebrated weekly Communion at the church, and the idea that Jesus was tangibly present in the celebration of this meal became our dominant narrative—though that is historically uncommon in a North American Pentecostal church. But at the church, I was always the one in the position of serving, not of being served. In a way I cannot entirely explain even now, one of the first things that shifted in me when my shipwreck happened was a desperate hunger for the tangible, tasteable presence of God through the experience of the Eucharist—now needing to be carried to the table, now needing to be served rather than to serve.

After I left the church I founded, I was so hungry to encounter God through the Lord's

Supper. In my own journey, my belief in the real presence of Christ in the Eucharist had long become the center of my faith. I was aching to find a place where I could receive the body and blood of Jesus every single week. So I shuffled into the big red doors of St. Peter's in uptown Charlotte a little awkwardly, a self-proclaimed hillbilly Pentecostal. The aesthetics of the place were foreign to me. Yet in a way, the simple artistry of the space made room for a sense of wonder, reverence, and otherness that made me feel at home in a place I did not precisely know but had longed for. I don't remember how long it took for me not to cry all the way through every service. I could close my eyes when the choir was singing behind us and actually feel like angels were singing over me. For all the ways some people may think of Episcopal churches in North America as rest homes for progressive white people, I can only tell you that St. Peter's is as ethnically diverse a church as I've been in. From the African-American male rector and white female associate rector, to the revolving door of beautiful faces in the pews around me, the church seems as integrated socioeconomically and culturally as it does ethnically.

I loved the warmth and compassion that seemed to radiate off the walls in there, and I loved being stone-cold anonymous. Off the grid from my evangelical circles, I felt completely safe to come as I was—to receive, to just be. I loved that it never felt like the church was trying to sell me anything. I loved that, really, nobody is fussed over at all—there just is not that kind of VIP treatment for anybody. The vibe is, "This is the kind of worship we do here, and you are welcome to come and do this with us . . . or not." The liturgy there does not try to coerce everyone into the same emotional experience, but in its corporate unity strangely creates space for us all to have a very personal experience of God. I have commented to friends that I have never actually prayed this much in church before.

With my own world feeling disordered and untethered, I was quite happy to be told when to kneel and when to sit and when to stand. I love that there was almost no space in the worship experience to spectate, because almost every moment invites (but not demands) participation. I had been in no position to tell my heart what to do. But because the church told my body what to do in worship, my heart was able to follow—sometimes. And that was enough.

It never felt like a tragedy there to not be the guy up front speaking—I'd been preaching since I was nineteen years old. That part is only gift. Ironically, as long-winded of a preacher as I was, I loved investing in a way of being and doing church where preaching really isn't all that central to begin with. In the Anglican tradition, preaching is never the main event. Preaching is only foreplay at most. All the weight of the liturgy lands on the Eucharist—preparing for it, receiving it, reflecting on it. I loved being part of a worship experience where so much emphasis is placed on the broken body and shed blood of Christ. I loved that I get to come and actually kneel at the altar, where someone looks me in the eye (when I hold my head up high enough for them to do so) and gives the elements to me. I cry around that altar week after week. When my heart is too overwhelmed, I slip out the side door after I receive the Eucharist, where a sweet older man and woman lay their hands on me and pray for me. After years of being in healing lines down at the front of the church waiting for evangelists to lay hands on me, I surely don't feel any shame or self-consciousness about just sliding into that back room for prayer. I go as often as I need to, without reservation. All this love and beauty, and they give the body and blood of Jesus away for free every week to anybody who wants it.

This Daily Bread

None of this helped me figure out, with any degree of clarity, where my life was headed. The prayer Jesus gave us to pray is, "Give us this day our daily bread."[2] There is no prayer for future bread. Like the manna God provided in the exodus story, there is bread that is supplied day by day, that cannot be kept or stored for the days ahead. It can only be received on this day, and then we will have to ask all over again the next day—learning to be dependent, at home in our creatureliness.

The word *this* is our only defense against the guilt of the past and the anxiety of the future. *This* daily bread. *This* chair you are sitting in. *This* song on the radio. *This* person sitting beside you now. *This* meal you are about to eat. We can't go back into the past and fix any old moments or propel ourselves into the future to find whatever is lurking there. All we can do is open our hands and our hearts to receive the gift of this meal, this day, this friend, this moment. *This* daily bread tethers us to the provision we have in this moment, however small—the only moment we have. "This" anchors us to the ground when we are floating, at least for a few fleeting seconds.

We need something more immediate than a memory of how God was revealed in the past, more immediate than mere hope that God will be revealed in the future. God can only be known and experienced in this moment—right here, right now. If we will attend to this moment, God will attend to us.

> If we will attend to this moment, God will attend to us.

Trying to find a way to attend to the moment myself, in that season where every step in every direction felt excruciating, I wrote this prayer as a way of tethering myself to the grace of this moment. I hope it can help you find the grace in whatever moment you're in right now:

> *I do not ask*
> *for some future bread.*
> *I do not ask*
> *for some lofty thing.*
> *I ask for nothing more,*
> *I ask for nothing less,*
> *than primal provision.*
> *For this, and this—only this.*
> *I do not ask for then.*
> *I do not ask for there.*
> *I do not ask for that.*
> *Only this meal—this moment.*
> *For this day, only*
> *for this, and this—only this.*

Holy Breath

Before my own shipwreck, I can't even recall a time when I ever really paid attention to my breathing. Which is, in a manner of speaking, a way of saying I wasn't paying attention to my life. It seems so clear now—how primal the connection is between Spirit and breath. No wonder in Hebrew and in Greek, the words for *spirit* and *breath* are the same. God is not just the source of breath; God *is* our breath—the Spirit fills our lungs even now, making each moment possible. "In him we live and move and have our being," Paul writes,[3] and this is one of the primary ways that God actively sustains all living things—through the gift of divine breath (is there any other kind?). Whatever kind of sea we may be swimming in (or drowning in), we are all somehow contained in the ocean of God himself, the source of all our being. If there is no other evidence in your life that God loves you, is there for you, or provides for you, consider the evidence of your own breath—each inhale and each exhale carrying with it the message that God is choosing you all over again, now, in this moment . . . in this breath.

And yet when the body is under duress, as I experienced often in my own shipwreck, it can feel like oxygen is in short supply. The very air that fills us with life, with possibility, with Spirit, is more difficult to access through labored, heavy breathing or short gasps of air. Returning to our breath is a way of returning to reality, the deeper reality than the crisis of our identity as creatures sustained by a God of love. Returning to our breath, being attentive to it, receiving the gift of it, is a primal way of returning to God himself. Do not let anyone ever convince you that only people with a certain spiritual pedigree have access to the Spirit. You know the Spirit is available to you, because of your constant access to the holy breath she gives you.

I was not connected to any such essential realities until the shipwreck made me feel like I was constantly on the verge of going under, and air did in fact feel in short supply. It is a long and wonderful story how a self-proclaimed hillbilly Pentecostal ended up flat on his back in a yoga studio, wearing an eye mask, lying under a blanket, smelling incense in the air—while my new friend James played a drum in the background. I mean, I once would have been suspicious of people who used incense in church! But driven by desperation, there I was, with a kind of tribal music playing in the background.

James is a Christian, though his breathing class is not explicitly Christian in its approach. He does talk about the connection between breath and spirit, how God fills us with holy breath, and how we can follow that breath where it leads us. I was so far broken open at that point, and my life felt so unmanageable—I was open to get to God anyhow, anyway, those days. Even if that meant a man in a tank top playing a drum was going to have to teach me how to breathe all over again. (I can't even imagine how much some of my friends reading this are going to want to travel back in time to stage an intervention.) But I felt astonishingly safe. So when all the pent-up grief in me came out, I didn't just cry; I wailed. I lost all track of myself. I'm glad they play the music loud, but then again, I was probably too far past myself to care what anybody else would have said. Every ounce of grief, of guilt, came out in what felt like an eternal kind of travail. And yet I felt so completely loved, somehow beheld so tenderly by the presence of Love himself. It was not Love in the abstract, but Love in the particular, the God revealed in Jesus of Nazareth, which is the only God I know. And how this God did meet me in that space. The deeper in I went, the more immersed I felt in the love of God. I had never experienced anything like it before.

I knew in my head that "in him we live and move and have our being."[4] I remembered Sister Anne, when I was on spiritual retreat, asking me to be mindful of God at work, holding together the dirt and rocks and sand and sky all around me when I walked the cliffs. But I don't think I ever *knew* experientially before that moment that God is not just a being; God is being itself. I don't think I ever really knew experientially the way David described God in the Psalms: "If I make my bed in the depths, you are there. If I rise on the wings of the dawn, if I settle on the far side of the sea, even there your hand will guide me, your right hand will hold me fast."[5] I don't think I ever really comprehended that this God literally could not be outrun, no matter where I fled or what I did. The very fact I exist means I exist in God and am sustained by God, literally with every single breath. The inescapable presence is the only reason I am able to be . . . anywhere, anytime, at all.

In case I have not made this sound sufficiently strange, I've had a consistent image in my mind the last few minutes of the new puppy my parents had bought—Gabi. While staying at their house—a thirty-six-year-old man feeling like a complete loser—them getting that sweet little dog had helped keep me alive. She didn't judge anything about my life or my heart. She just loved to see me come home to this place that was not my home, and she just wanted to be with me and play. The love of God was being manifested in the face of a dog that never takes her eyes off me, never wants me to leave, and always wants to draw me into life, laughter, and the wonder of the present moment.

I cried. Then I laughed. Then I cried-laughed, and laughed-cried. It was the experience I always wanted to find in the Pentecostal altar services. And to be clear, I believe in all of that, and I think there was in fact an encounter with the Spirit to be had in those places. It wasn't God who wasn't ready, but me. Before I was broken open by my own suffering, my own pain, even the pain I caused, I couldn't have dropped far enough from my head into my heart and body to enter fully into such a moment. Only in the experience of feeling bankrupt in every conceivable way—an absurd man living an absurd alternate version of my own life—did I reach the point of seeing I had no choice but to let go. How could there be any holding off that Presence now, when I couldn't even hold myself together?

I'm near delirious on the love of God, lying on the mat in a yoga studio, in an environment where there are no explicit markers of Christian worship at all. I had been lost in all the ways I never wanted, and thus finally in a posture where I could get lost in all the ways I always did want, but couldn't. James does little to direct the experience—he lets the Spirit work through us in the breathing. But a few moments later, I felt like God revealed to me an aspect of my life I was carrying in a way that was positively crushing me, consuming me . . . killing me. While it was deep, quiet, and entirely interior in the way I understand the voice of God to most often be, it was perhaps as clear as I felt I had ever heard the Spirit inside me. Echoing in the deepest chambers of my being, I heard these simple words: "You don't have to carry it anymore." Almost as soon as the phrase formed inside me, James bent down and gently whispered in my ear, out loud: "You don't have to carry it anymore, my brother."

Toward the end of the session, James bent down one more time and gently laid his hand on me. He was close enough to my head to where I could hear his voice softly above the music behind us.

He was speaking in tongues.

You certainly would not have to attend a class, like I did with James, to welcome in the presence of God through the holy breath you are taking right at this moment. The presence is available in the air all around you, waiting for you to pay attention, waiting for you to wake up to love. But part of the value of the experience for me is in the same way the consecrated

meal of the Eucharist helps me recognize the
fundamental ways that all meals are holy. The
consecrated, set-aside space for breathing helped
me become attentive to the Spirit available in all
of our breathing.

When we breathe—slowly, intentionally,
mindful of the source of life that fills our lungs
now—we return to who we really are. The sights
and sounds of the world around us now in its
clutter and clamor, of life in the city—and even
the sensory assault of a life that now feels under
water—all recede, and we return to the garden.
The Holy One communes with us still, creates
us still, sustains us still, breathes in us still. Being
attentive in just one breath—being open to the
Spirit in just one breath—is to open ourselves
up to the source of all life and the source of all
healing. The Spirit comes to us, riding on our
own breath, summoning us back home into the
quiet, gentle care of the One who keeps us alive
moment by moment, filling our lungs.

Sleeping

I have less to say about this than eating or breathing, because in a way, sleeping is the simplest of
these elemental blessings that call us back to life
and to the source of life in a shipwreck. We are

constantly overwhelmed with new data that tells us how many physiological and psychological benefits there are to sleeping, and how many risks there are associated with the lack of it. And yet, I'm quite sure most of us know this intuitively. The problem is not that we do not recognize our need for sleep or don't have a proper scientific understanding of its benefits, but that we just aren't actually sleeping. And during a time of shipwreck, there are so many, many reasons not to sleep.

Shipwrecked nights are the longest and slowest of nights. There is endless time to sit with your longing, your hurt, your desire, your despair, or your grief; there is endless time to replay what you did wrong and what you wish you had done differently. The loneliness, the isolation of the night—the sense of being caged inside your own skin—is profound. There are so many monsters, which we will look at later, that come out in the night.

I think often of the story of Elijah the prophet, who is on the run from people who want to kill him, now tired and hungry, and convinced he's the last man God has to stand for him on the earth. Paranoid and exhausted, he finally falls asleep—he literally takes a nap. And when he wakes up—look here! God supplied a biscuit. Oh, and wait—there are actually seven thousand other prophets he didn't know about! The food mattered. The knowledge that he was objectively not alone made a difference. But none of it was possible until he went to sleep. The world was not going to get any less threatening and he was not going to feel any more hopeful as long as he was sleep deprived.

When the shipwreck takes its toll on your body and your mind and you are utterly over-whelmed, sometimes you have to bravely pull the covers over your head and sleep it off. If you are sleeping fourteen hours a day and can't get up in the mornings, and you are depressed, someone can help you with that too—and there is never any shame in getting help to survive a shipwreck. It is essential. But I find most often in times of shipwreck, people suffer more from lack of sleep than from sleeping too much. The season is so long and so demanding that you get so used to living frantic, harried, panicked— there is no time for sleep. There is too much to worry about, too much to figure out!

There is no better medicine for the syndrome scientifically known as "God-doesn't-love-me-everyone-hates-me-I-just-want-to-die" than sleep. Sleep, in its own way, is an act of trust. We enter into the realm of the unconscious—vulnerable, where we cannot think, work, or wrangle. Even the most devout atheist enters into this act of surrender, this letting go into the night that lets us go into God as the one who sustains us, who keeps watch while we are no longer looking at our watches. And with or without our cooperation, when we sleep, God is at work to heal and restore what has been lost in the day's eternal battle with the sea. We take leave of the world we know to enter a world we do not know as well, and we are held. Frederick Buechner writes these words:

> Whether you're just or unjust, you have the innocence of a cat dozing under the stove. Whether you're old or young, homely or fair, you take on the serenity of marble. You have given up being in charge of your life. You have put yourself into the hands of the night.
>
> It is a rehearsal for the final laying down of arms, of course, when you trust yourself to the same unseen benevolence to see you through the dark and to wake you when the time comes— with new hope, new strength—into the return again of light.[6]

More pertinently, when sea and shipwreck have almost taken you under, "life is grace. Sleep is forgiveness. The night absolves. Darkness wipes the slate clean, not spotless to be sure, but clean enough for another day's chalking."[7]

I am not a doctor. But I am fairly convinced that anything from warm baths to special teas to boring fiction to Ambien is supremely better than not sleeping. If even in this moment, you are feeling so overwhelmed by the savage nature of your own life at sea, may I recommend that you not sit here long enough to ponder how you feel about the value of sleep as some sort of idea? This is one of the most tried and true ways to let God in—through a small and necessary act of letting go. If you can sleep now, even for a little while, you may well wake up to find a new set of glasses on the nightstand through which you might see the world and the storm outside in an entirely different way.

I know—you don't have much time, and you have other things to do. Set your clock if you absolutely must. But in this moment, God is waiting for you under the clock of your own slumber. Put the book down, and everything else you are carrying.

Sleep now. Trust now. Brother, sister, you don't have to carry it anymore.

Not tonight.

Tonight I will ask of you only one thing.

Please do not give up.

I know how dark it can be, how cold, how

desolate against the rocks and the elements. I know it seems, right now, that there can't possibly be true life again after shipwreck.

Please know this is not all there is. There is another wind, coming in slow on the wings of the morning, to hover over your still-flickering light, to fan you into fire, again.

Notes

Chapter One: Losing Your Ship without Losing Your Soul

1. Matthew 28.10.
2. Luke 10.18, NIV.
3. Luke 22.31–32.
4. Acts 27.34.

Chapter Three: Hold On, Let Go

1. Acts 27.20.
2. John 20.17, my paraphrase.
3. Acts 17.28.
4. Psalm 139.7–12.
5. Thomas Merton, *Love and Living* (New York: Farrar, Straus Giroux, 1979), 11–12.

Chapter Four: Eating, Breathing, Sleeping

1. Acts 27.33–38, NIV.
2. Matthew 6.11.
3. Acts 17.28.

4. Acts 17.28.

5. Psalm 139.8–10, NIV.

6. Frederick Buechner, *Whistling in the Dark: A Doubter's Dictionary* (San Francisco: HarperCollins, 1993), 114.

7. Frederick Buechner, *The Alphabet of Grace* (San Francisco: HarperCollins, 1970), 25.

How to Survive a Shipwreck

Help Is on the Way and Love Is Already Here

Jonathan Martin

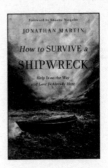

Life is turbulent. Disappointed dreams, broken relationships, identity crises, wounds from the past—there are so many ways life can send us crashing against the rocks.

Jonathan Martin draws from his own stories of failure and loss to find the love that can only be discovered on the bottom. *How to Survive a Shipwreck* is an invitation to trust the goodness of God and the resilience of your soul. Jonathan's clarion call is this: No matter how hard you've fallen, no matter how much you've been hurt, help is on the way—just when you need it most.

With visionary artistry and pastoral wisdom, Jonathan Martin reveals what we need to make it through uncharted waters, how we can use these defining experiences to live out of our depths, and why we'll no longer be able to go back to the half-life we once lived.

Available in stores and online!

ZONDERVAN®
.com